At YOUR age you're having a WHAT?!

The Advantages of Mature Maternity

by Rita Abrams
illustrated by Ellen Blonder

Library of Congress Cataloging-in-Publication Data

Abrams, Rita.
    At your age you're having a what?! : the advantages of mature
    maternity / Rita Abrams ; illustrated by Ellen Blonder.
        p.   cm.
    "A Thomas Dunne book."
    ISBN 0-312-05816-0
    1. Motherhood—United States—Humor.   2. Older parents—United
    States—Humor.   3. Mothers—United States—Humor.   I. Blonder,
    Ellen, 1950-   . II. Title.
    HQ759.A17   1991
    306.874'3'0207—dc20   90-28604
                                                               CIP

First published in the United States by Whatever Publishing, Inc.

10 9 8 7 6 5 4 3 2 1

To our babies,
who made this book inevitable.

Foreword...

Not so terribly long ago, a woman who made it through her twenties without marrying and bearing her full quota of babies was the object of grave concern to friends and relatives. And if, heaven forbid, her situation didn't change as she lumbered on toward thirty-five, the concern turned to pity.

Well, things have changed, as you probably know or you wouldn't have picked up this book. The phenomenon of "Mature Maternity" is spreading across the land faster than a fast food franchise.

In the hope of exploiting and capitalizing on this situation, we have conducted a half-baked, haphazard survey of women who have gone from Over the Hill to Over the Pill. Using extensive interviews and observations of the women pictured in this book, we have uncovered nearly sufficient evidence to support the following conclusions about Mature Maternity:

1. It's Easier.
2. It's Good for You.
3. It Makes You a Better Mother.

If after studying this book carefully, you do not agree with our conclusions, please do not under any circumstances contact us. We'll be too frazzled, disorganized, and over-burdened to deal with it.

R.J.A. & E.L.B.

Mature Maternity is EASIER because . . .

. . . you'll have no trouble getting your figure back.

NOT PREGNANT

PREGNANT

. . . you're in vogue.

. . . you get more respect from your obstetrician.

. . . you're more accepting of your body.

. . . you're not worried that maybe you should have waited for Mr. Right to come along. (You did—he never came.)

. . . you're better equipped financially to raise a child.

. . . you're rational enough to ignore all the myths and superstitions about pregnancy.

. . . you have fewer anxieties about the birth itself.

. . . thanks to advances in medical technology, you can find out the sex of your baby before its birth.

. . . your baby will be all the more special to those who had given up on your having one.

. . . you've sown all your wild oats and are ready to settle down to motherhood.

. . . your maturity will discourage unsolicited advice.

. . . you aren't tortured by fantasies of what you might have been if you hadn't gotten pregnant so early.

. . . you've conquered guilt.

. . . you're fully in touch with your body.

. . . you're a whiz at budgeting your time.

. . . you know how to react in emergencies.

. . . you've learned to disregard thoughtless remarks.

. . . you've established your career, and can return to it when you choose.

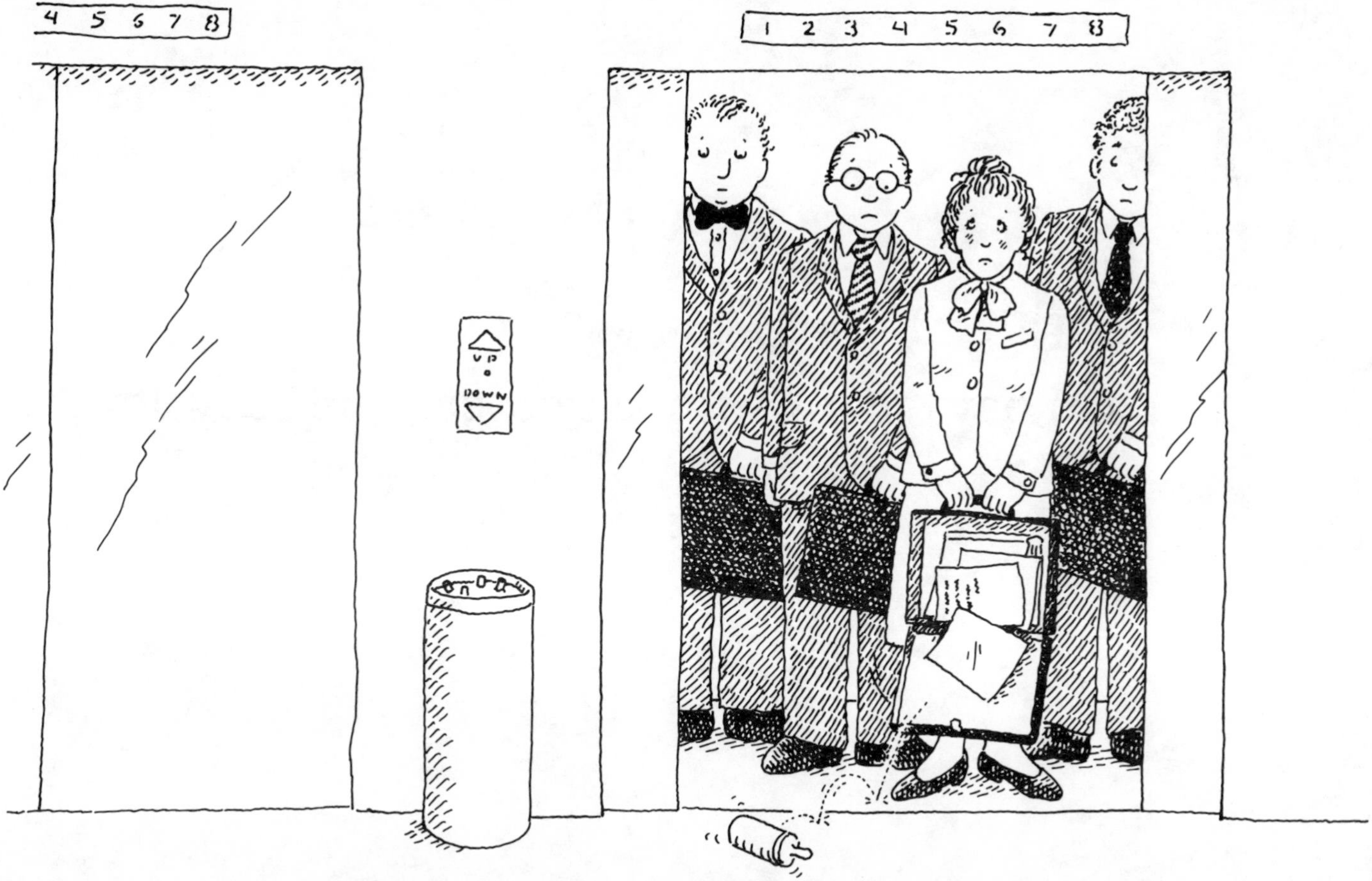
4 5 6 7 8
1 2 3 4 5 6 7 8
UP
DOWN

. . . you have more authority over your babysitter.

Mature Maternity is GOOD FOR YOU because . . .

. . . it ends those years of petty self-indulgence.

. . . it gives you the flattering benefits of today's maternity fashions.

. . . it forces you back into shape.

. . . it brings back the child in you.

. . . it gives you something to show for your cellulite.

. . . it puts you back in touch with nature.

. . . it adds depth to your personality.

. . . it takes your mind off aging.

. . . it provides living proof that you still have a sex life.

As a Mature Mother, You're a BETTER MOTHER
because . . .

. . . you're more conscientious about health and nutrition.

. . . you're more patient.

. . . you don't need to define yourself by your child's achievements.

. . . you've had more time to analyze the mistakes your mother made with you, in order not to repeat them.

. . . you have a richer literary background to share with your child.

. . . you're wise enough to let your child follow his or her own course.

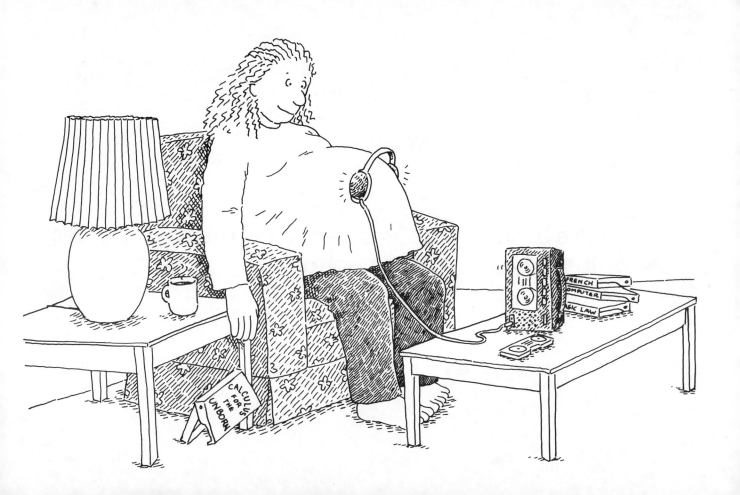

. . . you're in tune with your own instincts, and won't be confused by conflicting opinions.

. . . you're ideally suited to help your child develop a sense of responsibility.

. . . you're more secure in your identity, and therefore more able to separate your child's problems from your own.

. . . you're a better role model.

. . . you have a better grasp of appropriate activities for children.

. . . you believe in fostering independence.

. . . you're aware of the dangers of overprotecting your child.

. . . you're better prepared for your child's develop-
mental stages.

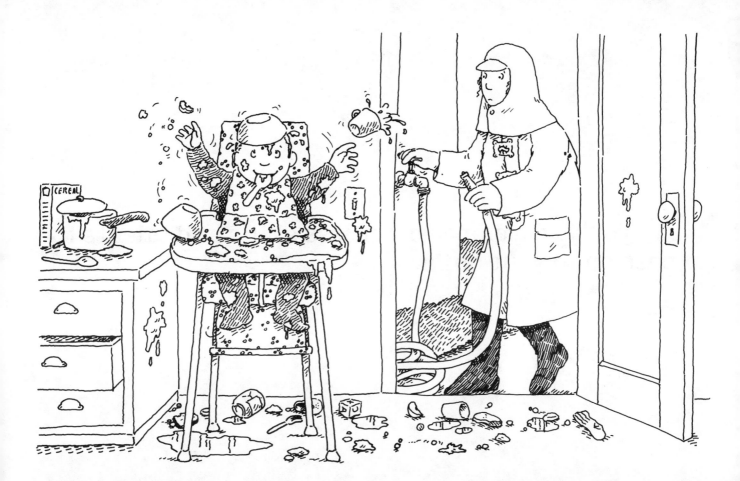

. . . you've developed countless skills and talents to pass on to your child.

. . . you know the necessity of setting limits.

. . . you have the resources to select the ideal childcare situation.

. . . you can devote yourself totally to this child, since you're too old to have any more.

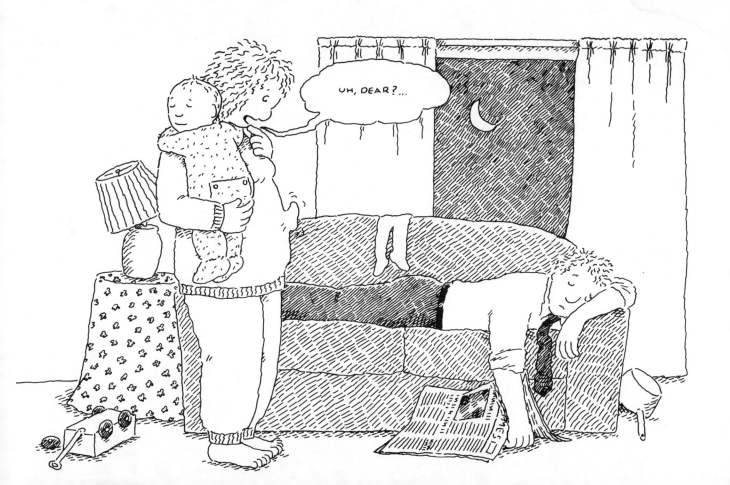

About the authors . . .

Rita Abrams is the former teacher whose record "Mill Valley," sung with the Strawberry Point Third Grade Class, became an international hit. Since then she has composed and produced music for numerous children's albums, videos, and films; written humor and greeting cards; and won an Emmy for scoring a TV documentary about Marin County, California, where she lives with her daughter Mia Rose, and their pet rat Froot Loop.

Ellen Blonder has been a freelance illustrator for seven years in the San Francisco area, working for a wide range of nationally known commercial and publishing clients. She and her husband Nick, an attorney, and their daughter Lisa Alexis live in Mill Valley, California.

Neither the author nor the illustrator considers herself personally to be an example of "Mature Maternity"—but each has recently collaborated with someone who is.